JEFFREY BENSON

CULTIVATING WEALTH BEYOND RICHES

JEFFREY BENSON

Copyright @ Jeffrey Benson

All rights reserved.

No part of this book may be reprinted, stored in a retrieval system or transmitted in any form or by any means without the prior written permission of the publisher, except by a reviewer who may quote brief passages in a review or be printed in a newspaper, magazine or journal.

ISBN: 9798345985250
Imprint: Independently published

CONTENTS

Chapter 1: The Seed of Prosperity

- The Concept of Prosperity: Defining prosperity beyond material wealth—encompassing health, happiness, and fulfillment.

- Mindset as the Fertile Ground: How a prosperity mindset serves as the foundation for wealth.

- The Importance of Vision: Setting clear, long-term goals as the seed from which wealth grows.

- Cultivating the Right Habits: Daily practices that nurture the seed of prosperity.

Chapter 2: Preparing the Soil: Financial Literacy

- Understanding Money: Basics of finance, budgeting, and saving.

- Debunking Money Myths: Common misconceptions about wealth and how they hinder prosperity.

- Building a Financial Foundation: Establishing emergency funds, good credit, and financial discipline.

- The Role of Education: Continuous learning and staying informed about financial matters.

Chapter 3: Planting the Seeds: Income Generation

- The Multiple Streams of Income Approach: Diversifying income sources for stability.

- Active vs. Passive Income: Exploring various avenues for earning, from careers to investments.

- Entrepreneurship as a Seed: How starting a business can plant a powerful seed for wealth.

- Leveraging Skills and Talents: Turning personal strengths into profitable ventures.

Chapter 4: Nurturing Growth: Investment Strategies

- The Power of Compounding: How investments grow over time.

- Real Estate and Property Investments: Creating long-term wealth through real estate.

- Stock Market Insights: Understanding stocks, bonds, and other investment vehicles.

- Risk Management: Balancing potential returns with risk and how to protect your investments.

Chapter 5: Weeding and Pruning: Overcoming Obstacles

- Debt Management: Strategies for paying off debt and staying debt-free.

- Overcoming Financial Setbacks: How to handle economic downturns, job loss, or failed investments.

- Avoiding Scams and Frauds: Recognizing and avoiding financial pitfalls.

- Emotional Intelligence in Wealth Building: Managing emotions that can derail financial plans.

Chapter 6: Harvesting Wealth: Realizing Financial Goals

- Setting and Achieving Milestones: Breaking down long-term financial goals into achievable steps.

- The Art of Saving and Spending Wisely: Finding a balance between enjoying wealth and sustaining it.

- Wealth vs. Riches: Understanding the difference and why it matters.

- Philanthropy and Giving Back: The role of generosity in a prosperous life.

Chapter 7: Sustaining the Harvest: Wealth Preservation

- Inheritance and Legacy Planning: How to ensure wealth benefits future generations.

- Insurance and Protection: Safeguarding assets through insurance and other protective measures.

- The Role of Taxes in Wealth Preservation: Understanding tax obligations and strategies for minimizing tax burdens.

- Continuous Reinvestment: Keeping wealth growing through smart reinvestment strategies.

Chapter 8: The Farmer's Toolbox: Essential Skills for Wealth Creation

- Time Management and Productivity: Maximizing time as a crucial resource.

- Networking and Relationships: Building and leveraging connections for wealth creation.

- Negotiation and Communication Skills: Essential for securing deals and opportunities.

- Resilience and Adaptability: Thriving in a constantly changing economic landscape.

Chapter 9: The Seasonal Cycles of Wealth

- Understanding Economic Cycles: Recognizing the phases of boom and bust in the economy.

- Adjusting Strategies with Seasons: How to adapt wealth-building strategies to economic conditions.

- Reaping During the Harvest Season: Identifying the right time to cash out or reinvest.

- Preparing for the Winter: Building a financial cushion for economic downturns.

Chapter 10: The Wealth Farmer's Legacy

- Building a Legacy of Wealth: Strategies for ensuring your wealth endures through generations.

- Teaching Financial Literacy to the Next Generation: Preparing your heirs to manage and grow wealth.

- Sustainable Wealth and Ethical Considerations: The moral and social responsibilities of wealth.

- Final Thoughts: The Wealth Farmer's Creed: Core principles to live by in the pursuit of lasting prosperity.

Chapter 11: Personal Stories of Harvesting Wealth

- Success Stories: Real-life examples of individuals who have successfully built and sustained wealth.

- Lessons Learned: What these stories teach us about perseverance, strategy, and mindset.

- Failures and Comebacks: Stories of those who faced setbacks but eventually found success.

Chapter 12: Your Path to Prosperity

- Creating Your Wealth Blueprint: A step-by-step guide to building your personalized wealth plan.

- Commitment and Discipline: The importance of staying the course.

- Reviewing and Adjusting the Plan: Regular check-ins and flexibility in your wealth strategy.

- Living a Life of Abundance: Embracing prosperity in all areas of life, not just financially.

This structure allows readers to follow a logical progression from understanding the principles of prosperity to the practical steps of wealth creation and finally to the preservation and legacy of wealth.

Chapter 1:
The Seed of Prosperity

The Concept of Prosperity

Prosperity is often misunderstood as merely the accumulation of wealth or material assets. While financial stability is a crucial component, true prosperity is a multifaceted concept that transcends money. It is an all-encompassing state of well-being that includes health, happiness, relationships, personal growth, and fulfillment. To truly "sow the seed of prosperity," one must first grasp this broader understanding and recognize that wealth is just one part of a prosperous life.

Health as a Cornerstone of Prosperity

Health is the foundation upon which all other aspects of prosperity are built. Without good health, the pursuit of wealth and success can be futile. Ancient wisdom often links health with wealth, as in the saying, "Health is wealth." This is not just a metaphor; it is a practical truth. A healthy body and mind are vital for the energy, focus, and resilience required to pursue and maintain prosperity.

Consider the story of Steve Jobs, co-founder of Apple Inc., who revolutionized technology and amassed enormous wealth. However, despite his success, Jobs faced significant health challenges, which eventually led to his untimely death. In his later years, Jobs famously reflected on the limits of wealth, stating that all the money in the world could not buy health and more time. His experience serves as a powerful reminder that health is an indispensable part of true prosperity.

Happiness and Fulfillment

Happiness is another critical aspect of prosperity. Research has shown that once basic needs are met, the correlation between wealth and happiness diminishes. This phenomenon, known as the "Easterlin Paradox," suggests that after reaching a certain income level, additional wealth does not significantly increase happiness. Instead, factors like relationships, purpose, and self-actualization play a more prominent role in overall well-being.

Consider the lives of billionaires who, despite their vast fortunes, often struggle with personal happiness. Some have spoken publicly about the hollow nature of wealth without fulfillment. Jim Carrey, a successful actor and comedian, once said, "I think everybody should get rich and famous and do everything they ever dreamed of so they can see that it's not the answer." His words underscore the idea that happiness cannot be bought and is a crucial element of prosperity.

Relationships and Social Connections

Strong, meaningful relationships contribute significantly to prosperity. These connections provide emotional support, opportunities for collaboration, and a sense of belonging. In his book Social Intelligence, psychologist Daniel Goleman highlights how social connections are not only vital for emotional well-being but also for physical health and success in life.

An illustrative example of this can be seen in the life of Warren Buffett, one of the world's wealthiest individuals. Buffett attributes much of his success not only to his financial acumen but also to the strong relationships he has cultivated over the years. He often emphasizes the importance of surrounding oneself with people who are smarter and more talented, and he values the friendships and partnerships that have helped him in his career.

Personal Growth and Self-Actualization

The final piece of the prosperity puzzle is personal growth and self-actualization. Prosperity involves continuous learning, self-improvement, and striving toward one's full potential. The concept of self-actualization, popularized by psychologist Abraham Maslow, refers to the realization of one's talents, potential, and purpose in life. It is the pinnacle of Maslow's hierarchy of needs, symbolizing the ultimate form of prosperity.

Consider the example of Oprah Winfrey, who rose from poverty to become one of the most influential and wealthy individuals in the world. Oprah's journey to prosperity was not just about accumulating wealth but also about pursuing her passion for media, empowering others, and continuously growing as an individual. Her story exemplifies how personal growth and self-actualization are integral to true prosperity.

Mindset as the Fertile Ground

Just as fertile soil is essential for a seed to grow, the right mindset is crucial for the seed of prosperity to take root and flourish. A prosperity mindset is characterized by positive thinking, a growth-oriented perspective, resilience, and an abundance mentality. It is the foundation upon which all other efforts to achieve prosperity are built.

The Power of Positive Thinking

Positive thinking is not about ignoring challenges or being blindly optimistic; it is about approaching situations with a constructive attitude and believing in the possibility of success. Studies in psychology have shown that individuals with a positive mindset are more likely to persevere in the face of obstacles and are generally more successful in achieving their goals.

One notable example is the story of Thomas Edison, the inventor of the light bulb. Edison famously failed thousands of times before successfully inventing the incandescent light bulb. When asked about his repeated failures, he reportedly said, "I have not failed. I've just found 10,000 ways that won't work." Edison's positive mindset and belief in eventual success were crucial in his journey toward prosperity.

Growth Mindset vs. Fixed Mindset

The concept of a growth mindset, developed by psychologist Carol Dweck, is essential for cultivating prosperity. A growth mindset is the belief that abilities and intelligence can be developed through effort, learning, and persistence. In contrast, a fixed mindset is the belief that these traits are innate and unchangeable.

Dweck's research has shown that individuals with a growth mindset are more likely to embrace challenges, learn from criticism, and persist in the face of setbacks—all of which are vital for achieving prosperity. An illustration of this can be found in the lives of successful entrepreneurs like Elon Musk, who are known for their relentless pursuit of innovation and their willingness to learn from failure. Musk's mindset allows him to see challenges as opportunities for growth rather than insurmountable obstacles.

Resilience in the Face of Adversity

Resilience, or the ability to bounce back from adversity, is a key component of a prosperity mindset. Life is unpredictable, and challenges are inevitable. However, those who possess resilience can navigate these challenges and emerge stronger. Resilience is not about avoiding difficulties but about developing the mental and emotional strength to overcome them.

Consider the story of J.K. Rowling, the author of the Harry Potter series. Before achieving literary success, Rowling faced numerous rejections from publishers and struggled with poverty and depression. Despite these challenges, she remained resilient, continuing to write and submit her work until she finally achieved success. Her story is a testament to the power of resilience in the pursuit of prosperity.

The Abundance Mentality

An abundance mentality is the belief that there is enough success, wealth, and opportunities to go around. This mindset contrasts with a scarcity mentality, which views resources as limited and leads to competition, fear, and envy. An abundance mentality fosters collaboration, generosity, and a positive approach to wealth-building.

One illustrative example is the philanthropic efforts of Bill Gates, co-founder of Microsoft. Gates, who once held the title of the world's richest person, has pledged to give away the majority of his wealth through the Bill & Melinda Gates Foundation. His abundance mentality not only guides his approach to wealth but also inspires others to contribute to the greater good. Gates' belief in the power of giving and collaboration is a clear demonstration of how an abundance mentality can be a fertile ground for true prosperity.

The Importance of Vision

Vision is the seed from which all prosperity grows. It provides direction, purpose, and motivation. Without a clear vision, efforts can be scattered, and opportunities may be missed. Vision is about seeing the bigger picture and understanding the long-term impact of daily actions. It involves setting clear, long-term goals and developing a plan to achieve them.

Defining Your Vision

To sow the seed of prosperity, one must first define a clear vision. This vision should be specific, actionable, and aligned with one's values and passions. It should encompass all aspects of prosperity, including financial goals, personal growth, relationships, and overall well-being.

A well-defined vision acts as a roadmap, guiding decisions and actions toward the desired outcome. Consider the example of Martin Luther King Jr., whose vision of racial equality and justice in America was a powerful force that drove his actions and inspired millions. King's vision was clear, compelling, and deeply rooted in his values, making it a pivotal element in the civil rights movement.

The Role of Visualization

Visualization is a powerful tool for turning vision into reality. It involves mentally picturing the achievement of goals and the realization of one's vision. Research in psychology and neuroscience has shown that visualization can enhance motivation, increase focus, and improve performance.

Elite athletes, for example, often use visualization techniques to mentally rehearse their performances. Olympic swimmer Michael Phelps, one of the most decorated athletes in history, has spoken about the importance of visualization in his training. By mentally rehearsing his races, Phelps prepared himself not only physically but also mentally, ensuring that his vision of winning gold medals became a reality.

Setting SMART Goals

A vision without actionable goals is just a dream. To make a vision a reality, it is essential to set SMART goals—Specific, Measurable, Achievable, Relevant, and Time-bound. SMART goals break down the vision into manageable steps and provide a clear path forward.

For example, if the vision is to achieve financial independence, a SMART goal might be to save a certain percentage of income each month, invest in a diversified portfolio, and achieve a specific net worth within a defined timeframe. By setting SMART goals, individuals can measure progress, stay motivated, and make necessary adjustments along the way.

The Power of Long-Term Thinking

Long-term thinking is critical in the pursuit of prosperity. It involves looking beyond immediate gratification and focusing on the bigger picture. This approach requires patience, discipline, and a willingness to delay short-term pleasures for long-term gains.

Consider the story of Jeff Bezos, the founder of Amazon. Bezos is known for his long-term thinking and willingness to invest in ideas that may not yield immediate returns.

Jeff Bezos, the founder of Amazon, is a prime example of how long-term thinking and a willingness to invest in ideas that may not yield immediate returns can drive success. Bezos has always emphasized the importance of thinking years, even decades, ahead. This mindset has been a cornerstone of Amazon's growth and dominance in multiple industries.

One of the most notable aspects of Bezos's approach is his focus on customer obsession and innovation. From the very beginning, he understood that prioritizing customer satisfaction would create a loyal customer base, which in turn would fuel long-term growth. This led to the creation of Amazon Prime, a service that initially seemed like a financial risk but ultimately revolutionized customer loyalty and transformed the e-commerce landscape.

Moreover, Bezos's willingness to invest in experimental projects has paid off in significant ways. For example, Amazon Web Services (AWS) started as an internal tool to manage the company's growing infrastructure but later evolved into a leading cloud computing service that now generates substantial revenue for Amazon. This success story underscores the importance of not just focusing on short-term profits but being open to exploring new ideas that could have far-reaching impacts.

Another critical aspect of Bezos's mindset is his emphasis on adaptability and embracing failure as a part of the innovation process. He has often spoken about the need to experiment, take risks, and accept that not all ventures will succeed. This approach has allowed Amazon to stay at the forefront of technological advancements and continuously expand into new markets, such as with the acquisition of Whole Foods and the development of AI-driven products like Alexa.

In essence, Jeff Bezos's long-term thinking, customer-centric approach, and willingness to invest in ideas with uncertain outcomes have been key drivers behind Amazon's success. His story illustrates the power of a visionary mindset in building a company that not only thrives in the present but also positions itself for continued growth in the future.

Chapter 2:

Preparing the Soil: Financial Literacy

Understanding Money: Basics of Finance, Budgeting, and Saving

Financial literacy is the cornerstone of personal prosperity. It encompasses the knowledge and skills needed to make informed financial decisions, manage money effectively, and achieve long-term financial goals. At its core, financial literacy involves understanding the fundamentals of finance, budgeting wisely, and cultivating the habit of saving.

The Basics of Finance

Finance is the management of money and includes activities such as investing, borrowing, budgeting, saving, and planning for retirement. Understanding these fundamental concepts is essential for making sound financial decisions.

1. Budgeting: Budgeting is the process of creating a plan for how to spend and save money. It helps individuals allocate resources effectively, prioritize expenses, and track financial goals. A budget typically includes income, expenses, savings, and debt repayment.

   - Example: Imagine Sarah, a recent college graduate starting her career. By creating a budget, Sarah can allocate a portion of her income toward rent, utilities, groceries, student loan payments, and savings for future goals like buying a home or traveling.

2. Saving: Saving involves setting aside money for future use rather than spending it immediately. It is a fundamental habit that enables individuals to build wealth, create financial security, and prepare for unexpected expenses.

- Example: John, a middle-aged professional, saves a percentage of his income each month in an emergency fund and retirement accounts. This disciplined approach ensures he has financial stability and can weather economic downturns or unforeseen events.

3. Investing: Investing involves putting money into financial products with the expectation of generating returns over time. It plays a crucial role in wealth accumulation and achieving long-term financial goals such as retirement planning or funding education.

- Example: Maria invests in stocks, bonds, and mutual funds through her retirement accounts and brokerage account. By diversifying her investments and staying informed about market trends, Maria aims to grow her wealth and achieve financial independence.

Debunking Money Myths: Common Misconceptions About Wealth

Misconceptions about money and wealth can hinder individuals from achieving financial prosperity. By debunking these myths and understanding the truth behind financial principles, individuals can make informed decisions and take proactive steps toward financial well-being.

1. Myth: Wealth is Only for the Lucky or Inherited

Reality: While inheritances and windfalls can contribute to wealth, many individuals achieve financial success through hard work, strategic planning, and financial discipline.

- Example: Elon Musk, the CEO of Tesla and SpaceX, built his wealth through entrepreneurship, innovation, and strategic investments rather than inheritance. His journey demonstrates that wealth can be earned through dedication and vision.

2. Myth: Debt is Always Bad

Reality: Not all debt is detrimental. Strategic borrowing such as for education or a mortgage, can be an investment for future earnings and asset acquisition.

- Example: Taking out a student loan to finance higher education can lead to increased earning potential and career opportunities, outweighing the initial debt burden. Responsible debt management is key to leveraging borrowing for long-term financial gain.

3. Myth: You Need a High Income to Build Wealth

Reality: While a higher income can accelerate wealth accumulation, individuals with modest incomes can still achieve financial security through budgeting, saving, and investing wisely.

- Example: Dave Ramsey, a financial expert, emphasizes that financial security is more about managing money effectively than earning a high income. By living within their means, even individuals with lower incomes can build wealth over time.

4. Myth: Investing is Risky and Complicated

Reality: While all investments carry some degree of risk, informed decision-making, diversification, and long-term planning can mitigate risks and optimize returns.

- Example: Warren Buffett, renowned investor and CEO of Berkshire Hathaway, advocates for a simple and disciplined approach to investing. His strategy focuses on acquiring quality assets at reasonable prices and holding them for the long term, demonstrating that investing can be both straightforward and rewarding.

Building a Financial Foundation: Establishing Emergency Funds, Good Credit, and Financial Discipline

A strong financial foundation is essential for weathering economic uncertainties, seizing opportunities, and achieving long-term financial goals. It involves establishing emergency funds, maintaining good credit, and practicing financial discipline.

1. Emergency Funds: An emergency fund is a savings account reserved for unexpected expenses such as medical emergencies, car repairs, or job loss. It serves as a financial safety net and prevents individuals from relying on high-interest debt during emergencies.

   - Example: Emily, a young professional, sets aside three to six months' worth of living expenses in an emergency fund. This precautionary measure provides peace of mind and financial resilience in the face of unforeseen circumstances.

2. Good Credit: Building and maintaining good credit is crucial for accessing favorable interest rates on loans, securing housing rentals, and qualifying for credit cards. It involves paying bills on time, managing debt responsibly, and monitoring credit reports regularly.

   - Example: James diligently monitors his credit score and reports, ensuring they accurately reflect his financial history. By maintaining a high credit score, James enhances his financial credibility and increases his access to financial opportunities.

3. Financial Discipline: Financial discipline entails making deliberate choices about spending, saving, and investing to align with long-term financial goals. It requires self-control, consistency, and the ability to prioritize financial stability over short-term gratification.

   - Example: Sarah practices financial discipline by creating a monthly budget, limiting discretionary spending, and automating savings contributions. Her disciplined approach allows her to achieve financial milestones and plan for future aspirations.

   The Role of Education: Continuous Learning and Staying Informed About Financial Matters

Continuous learning about financial principles, trends, and strategies is essential for adapting to changing economic landscapes, making informed decisions, and optimizing financial outcomes.

1. Financial Literacy Programs: Formal education programs, workshops, and online courses provide individuals with foundational knowledge about money management, investing, retirement planning, and wealth accumulation strategies.

   - Example: Jack attends a financial literacy workshop hosted by a local community center. Through interactive sessions and expert guidance, Jack learns about budgeting techniques, investment options, and retirement savings strategies.

2. Self-Education: Reading books, articles, and blogs written by financial experts can expand individuals' understanding of complex financial concepts, investment opportunities, and economic trends.

   - Example: Emma subscribes to financial newsletters and follows reputable financial bloggers to stay updated on market developments, investment insights, and personal finance tips. Her commitment to self-education enhances her financial literacy and decision-making skills.

3. Financial Advisors: Consulting with certified financial advisors or planners can provide personalized guidance, portfolio management strategies, and retirement planning solutions tailored to individuals' financial goals and risk tolerance.

   - Example: Mark schedules a consultation with a certified financial planner to review his investment portfolio, assess retirement readiness, and develop a comprehensive financial plan. The advisor's expertise and recommendations empower Mark to make informed decisions and achieve financial security.

The explanations provide a comprehensive exploration of financial literacy, covering the fundamentals of finance, debunking common money myths, establishing a solid financial foundation, and emphasizing the importance of continuous learning in financial matters. Understanding these principles equips individuals with the knowledge and skills necessary to navigate their financial journey effectively and pursue long-term prosperity.

Chapter 3:

Planting the Seeds: Income Generation

The Multiple Streams of Income Approach: Diversifying Income Sources for Stability

Diversifying income sources is a strategy that involves generating revenue from multiple streams to reduce financial dependency on a single source and increase overall stability and resilience. By diversifying income, individuals can mitigate risks, seize new opportunities, and enhance their financial security.

Understanding Multiple Streams of Income

1. Primary Income: Primary income refers to earnings from a primary job or career. It is the main source of income that sustains daily living expenses, financial obligations, and savings goals.

 - Example: Sarah works as a marketing manager for a tech company, earning a steady salary that covers her living expenses and provides financial stability.

2. Secondary Income: Secondary income includes earnings from part-time jobs, freelance work, consulting gigs, or side businesses. It supplements primary income and provides additional cash flow.

 - Example: John, a software engineer, freelances as a web developer in the evenings and weekends, earning extra income that he uses to build savings and invest in stocks.

3. Passive Income: Passive income is revenue generated with minimal ongoing effort or active involvement. It includes rental income from real estate properties, dividends from investments, royalties from intellectual property, and affiliate marketing earnings.

- Example: Emma invests in dividend-paying stocks and receives quarterly dividend payments. This passive income stream supplements her salary and grows her wealth over time.

4. Portfolio Income: Portfolio income derives from investment activities such as buying and selling stocks, bonds, mutual funds, and other financial assets. It includes capital gains from asset appreciation and interest income from bonds.

  - Example: Mark invests in a diversified portfolio of stocks and bonds, earning portfolio income through dividends and capital gains. His investment strategy aims to generate long-term growth and income.

Benefits of Diversifying Income Sources

- Risk Mitigation: Diversifying income reduces reliance on a single source, protecting against job loss, economic downturns, or industry-specific challenges.

- Income Stability: Multiple streams of income provide consistent cash flow, even if one source fluctuates or temporarily declines.

- Opportunity for Growth: Diversification opens doors to new income opportunities, skills development, and potential career advancements.

- Financial Freedom: Over time, diversified income streams can lead to financial independence, allowing individuals to pursue personal passions, retire early, or explore new ventures without financial constraints.

Active vs. Passive Income: Exploring Various Avenues for Earning

Understanding the distinction between active and passive income is crucial for developing a comprehensive income generation strategy. Active income requires ongoing effort and time investment, while passive income generates revenue with minimal ongoing effort once established.

Active Income

1. Employment Income: Salary or wages earned from a job or career requiring active participation, skills, and time commitment.

 - Example: Tom works full-time as a financial analyst at a corporate firm, earning a salary based on his experience and expertise in financial analysis.

2. Consulting and Freelancing: Providing specialized services or expertise on a contract basis to clients or businesses in exchange for fees or hourly rates.

 - Example: Lisa, a graphic designer, freelance for various clients, creating branding materials, logos, and marketing collateral on a project basis.

3. Commission-Based Sales: Earning income through sales commissions by selling products, services, or subscriptions on behalf of a company or as an independent sales representative.

 - Example: Mike works as a real estate agent, earning commissions from property sales and rental transactions based on successful deals closed.

Passive Income

1. Rental Income: Earnings from leasing residential or commercial properties to tenants in exchange for rent payments. Rental income provides recurring cash flow and potential property appreciation.

 - Example: Emily invests in rental properties, earning passive income from monthly rental payments and property value appreciation over time.

2. Dividend Income: Regular payments distributed to shareholders by companies as a portion of their profits. Dividends are a form of passive income generated from stock ownership.

  - Example: Jack owns shares in dividend-paying companies, earning quarterly dividend payments based on his stock holdings and company profitability.

3. Royalties and Licensing Fees: Income earned from licensing intellectual property, such as books, music, patents, or software, to third parties for commercial use.

  - Example: Sarah, an author, earns royalties from book sales and licensing agreements with publishers for digital distribution rights.

Entrepreneurship as a Seed: How Starting a Business Can Plant a Powerful Seed for Wealth

Entrepreneurship involves launching and operating a business venture with the goal of generating profit and creating value. It is a powerful avenue for income generation, wealth creation, innovation, and economic growth. Successful entrepreneurs identify opportunities, solve problems, and deliver products or services that meet market demand.

Key Elements of Entrepreneurship

1. Identifying Opportunities: Entrepreneurs identify gaps or inefficiencies in the market and develop innovative solutions or products to address customer needs or pain points.

  - Example: Steve Jobs and Steve Wozniak founded Apple Inc. to develop and sell personal computers, revolutionizing the technology industry and consumer electronics market.

2. Business Planning and Execution: Effective entrepreneurship requires strategic planning, market research, feasibility analysis, and a well-defined business plan to guide operations and growth.

   - Example: Jeff Bezos launched Amazon as an online bookstore, strategically expanding its product offerings and services to become the world's largest e-commerce retailer.

3. Risk Management and Adaptability: Entrepreneurship involves managing risks, navigating challenges, and adapting to market dynamics, competition, and changing consumer preferences.

   - Example: Elon Musk founded SpaceX to reduce space transportation costs and enable the colonization of Mars, overcoming technical challenges and regulatory hurdles in the aerospace industry.

4. Scaling and Growth: Successful entrepreneurs scale their businesses by expanding operations, increasing market share, entering new markets, and diversifying revenue streams.

   - Example: Mark Zuckerberg founded Facebook as a social networking platform for college students, scaling it into a global technology company with billions of users and diversified digital services.

Benefits of Entrepreneurship

- **Wealth Creation**: Entrepreneurs have the potential to generate substantial wealth through business ownership, equity ownership, and capital appreciation.

- **Innovation and Creativity**: Entrepreneurship fosters innovation, creativity, and technological advancements that drive economic growth and societal progress.

- **Job Creation**: Successful businesses create job opportunities, employ workers, and contribute to local economies through economic activity and tax revenues.

- **Personal Fulfillment**: Entrepreneurship allows individuals to pursue their passions, interests, and vision, contributing to personal fulfillment, autonomy, and professional satisfaction.

Leveraging Skills and Talents: Turning Personal Strengths into Profitable Ventures

Leveraging skills and talents involves identifying personal strengths, expertise, knowledge, and unique capabilities that can be monetized or turned into profitable ventures. By capitalizing on strengths, individuals can create income opportunities, build competitive advantage, and enhance career prospects.

Identifying Personal Strengths

1. Skills and Expertise: Individuals possess skills, knowledge, and expertise acquired through education, training, work experience, and personal interests.

   - Example: Julia, a certified public accountant (CPA), leverages her accounting skills and expertise to offer freelance tax preparation services during tax season.

2. Creativity and Innovation: Creativity involves generating original ideas, solutions, products, or services that add value, solve problems, or meet market demand.

   - Example: Adam, a graphic designer, showcases his creative talents by designing custom logos, branding materials, and digital illustrations for clients and businesses.

3. Technical Proficiency: Technical proficiency includes proficiency in software applications, programming languages, digital tools, and technical skills relevant to specific industries or professions.

  - Example: Sarah, a software engineer, leverages her programming skills and technical expertise to develop mobile applications, software solutions, and digital platforms for clients and businesses.

4. Communication and Leadership: Communication skills and leadership qualities enable individuals to influence, motivate, collaborate, and lead teams effectively within organizations or entrepreneurial ventures.

  - Example: Michael, a marketing manager, leverages his communication skills and leadership qualities to develop strategic marketing campaigns, manage client relationships, and drive business growth.

Monetizing Skills and Talents

1. Freelancing and Consulting: Freelancing involves offering specialized services, expertise, or skills on a contract basis to clients, businesses, or organizations in exchange for fees or hourly rates.

  - Example: Lisa, a freelance writer, monetizes her writing skills by producing content, articles, blog posts, and marketing materials for clients, publishers, and digital platforms.

2. Teaching and Training: Teaching and training involve sharing knowledge, skills, expertise, and educational content with students, learners, or professionals through workshops, courses, seminars, or online platforms.

  - Example: John, a certified personal trainer, monetizes his fitness expertise by offering personalized training programs, fitness coaching, and nutritional counseling services to clients and athletes.

3. Digital and Creative Services: Digital and creative services include providing graphic design, web development, digital marketing, content creation, photography, videography, and creative services to clients and businesses.

- Example: Emma, a digital marketer, monetizes her digital marketing skills by developing digital marketing strategies, managing social media campaigns, and optimizing online advertising for clients and brands.

4. Artistic and Performing Arts: Artistic and performing arts involve creating original artworks, paintings, sculptures, crafts, music compositions, performances, exhibitions, and creative works for sale.

- Example: Jack, a professional musician, monetizes his

skills and talents by performing live concerts, recording music albums, licensing music for films and commercials, and offering music lessons to aspiring musicians and students.

Various strategies for income generation have been emphasized, detailing the importance of diversifying income sources, understanding the differences between active and passive income, harnessing entrepreneurship as a powerful wealth-building tool, and leveraging personal skills and talents for profitable ventures. By adopting a multi-faceted approach to income generation, individuals can enhance financial stability, create opportunities for wealth accumulation, and achieve long-term prosperity. The next chapters will delve deeper into strategies for wealth preservation, investment growth, and sustainable financial planning to further empower readers on their journey to financial independence and success.

Chapter 4:

Nurturing Growth: Investment Strategies

Investing is a fundamental strategy for building wealth, achieving financial goals, and securing long-term financial independence. This chapter explores key investment principles, strategies, and insights to empower individuals to make informed investment decisions and maximize returns while managing risks effectively.

The Power of Compounding: How Investments Grow Over Time

Compounding is a powerful concept in investing that allows money to grow exponentially over time. It involves earning returns on both the initial principal and the accumulated earnings from previous periods. The longer the investment horizon and the higher the rate of return, the greater the potential for wealth accumulation through compounding.

Understanding Compounding

1. Compound Interest: Compound interest is the interest earned on the initial principal and also on the accumulated interest from previous periods. It accelerates wealth growth by reinvesting earnings to generate additional income over time.

  - Example: Sarah invests $10,000 in a savings account with an annual interest rate of 5%. After one year, her investment grows to $10,500. In the second year, she earns interest not only on the initial $10,000 but also on the $500 interest earned in the first year.

2. Time Horizon: The longer the investment period, the more significant the impact of compounding. Starting early and allowing investments to compound over decades can significantly increase wealth and retirement savings.

  - Example: John starts investing $5,000 annually in a retirement account at age 25. By age 65, his investments have grown substantially due to compounding, allowing him to retire comfortably.

3. Rate of Return: Higher rates of return amplify the effects of compounding. Investments with higher growth potential, such as stocks or equity funds, can generate higher long-term returns through compounding.

   - Example: Emily invests in a diversified portfolio of stocks with an average annual return of 8%. Over time, the compounding effect accelerates her portfolio growth and wealth accumulation.

Real Estate and Property Investments: Creating Long-Term Wealth Through Real Estate

Real estate investments offer opportunities for wealth creation, passive income generation, and portfolio diversification. Investing in residential, commercial, or rental properties can provide rental income, property appreciation, tax benefits, and inflation protection over the long term.

Types of Real Estate Investments

1. Residential Properties: Investing in single-family homes, condominiums, or multifamily residences for rental income or property appreciation.

   - Example: Mark purchases a duplex property and rents out one unit while living in the other. Rental income from tenants covers mortgage payments and generates passive income.

2. Commercial Properties: Investing in office buildings, retail centers, industrial warehouses, or mixed-use developments for lease to businesses or tenants.

   - Example: Sarah invests in commercial real estate properties leased to corporate tenants. Monthly lease payments provide stable rental income and potential capital appreciation.

3. Real Estate Investment Trusts (REITs): REITs are publicly traded companies that own, operate, or finance income-producing real estate. Investing in REITs allows individuals to gain exposure to real estate assets without directly owning physical properties.

- Example: Jack invests in REITs listed on stock exchanges, earning dividends from rental income and capital gains from property appreciation within the REIT portfolio.

4. Real Estate Crowd funding: Crowd funding platforms enable individuals to invest in real estate projects or properties alongside other investors. It provides access to diversified real estate investments with lower capital requirements.

- Example: Emily participates in a real estate crowdfunding platform, pooling funds with other investors to finance a commercial property development project. She earns returns through rental income and property resale.

Stock Market Insights: Understanding Stocks, Bonds, and Other Investment Vehicles

The stock market offers opportunities for capital growth, dividend income, and wealth accumulation through equity investments. Understanding different investment vehicles, risk tolerance, and investment strategies is essential for navigating stock market dynamics and optimizing investment returns.

Types of Investment Vehicles

1. Stocks: Stocks represent ownership in a publicly traded company. Investors purchase shares of stock to gain exposure to company growth, profitability, and potential dividend payments.

- Example: Tom invests in technology stocks of innovative companies known for growth potential and technological advancements. He diversifies his portfolio to mitigate risks and capitalize on market opportunities.

2. Bonds: Bonds are debt securities issued by governments, corporations, or municipalities to raise capital. Bondholders receive periodic interest payments and repayment of principal at maturity.

  - Example: Lisa invests in government bonds issued by stable economies with low default risk. Bonds provide predictable income and capital preservation within her investment portfolio.

3. Mutual Funds: Mutual funds pool money from multiple investors to invest in a diversified portfolio of stocks, bonds, or other securities managed by professional fund managers.

  - Example: Mike invests in a diversified mutual fund that tracks a stock market index, such as the S&P 500. Mutual funds offer diversification, professional management, and liquidity for investors.

4. Exchange-Traded Funds (ETFs): ETFs are investment funds traded on stock exchanges, mirroring the performance of a specific index, sector, commodity, or asset class.

  - Example: Emma invests in ETFs that track the global real estate market, providing exposure to diversified real estate assets and potential dividend income from REITs.

Investment Strategies and Considerations

1. Asset Allocation: Balancing investments across different asset classes, such as stocks, bonds, real estate, and cash equivalents, to achieve diversification and optimize risk-adjusted returns.

- Example: John diversifies his investment portfolio by allocating assets across stocks, bonds, and real estate investments based on his risk tolerance, investment goals, and time horizon.

2. Risk Tolerance: Assessing individual risk tolerance, investment objectives, and time horizon to select investment vehicles aligned with financial goals and risk management strategies.

   - Example: Sarah, a conservative investor nearing retirement, prioritizes capital preservation and income stability by investing in low-risk bonds and dividend-paying stocks.

3. Long-Term Investing: Adopting a long-term investment approach to capitalize on market growth, compounding returns, and economic cycles while maintaining a disciplined investment strategy.

   - Example: Mark practices dollar-cost averaging by investing a fixed amount regularly in mutual funds. Over time, he benefits from market fluctuations and long-term growth potential.

Risk Management: Balancing Potential Returns with Risk and How to Protect Your Investments

Risk management is essential for safeguarding investments, preserving capital, and mitigating potential financial losses. Understanding different types of investment risks, implementing diversification strategies, and utilizing risk management tools are critical for protecting investments and achieving sustainable growth.

Types of Investment Risks

1. Market Risk: Market risk refers to the possibility of investment losses due to market volatility, economic downturns, geopolitical events, or sector-specific challenges.

- Example: Lisa **diversifies** her investment portfolio across stocks, bonds, and real estate to mitigate market risk and minimize potential losses during market downturns.

2. Interest Rate Risk: Interest rate risk affects bond prices and fixed-income investments. Rising interest rates may decrease bond prices, impacting investment returns and income generation.

- Example: Mike monitors interest rate trends and adjusts his bond portfolio duration to minimize interest rate risk exposure and optimize bond investment returns.

3. Inflation Risk: Inflation risk reduces purchasing power over time, eroding the value of money and investment returns. Investing in inflation-protected securities or real assets helps hedge against inflationary pressures.

- Example: Emma allocates a portion of her investment portfolio to inflation-indexed bonds and commodities to preserve purchasing power and maintain investment value.

4. Liquidity Risk: Liquidity risk arises when investments cannot be sold or converted into cash quickly without significant price discounts. Maintaining a diversified portfolio with liquid assets enhances liquidity and financial flexibility.

- Example: Jack maintains an emergency fund and liquid investments in money market funds to meet short-term financial needs and mitigate liquidity risk.

Risk Management Strategies

1. Diversification: Spreading investments across different asset classes, industries, regions, and investment vehicles to reduce concentration risk and enhance portfolio resilience.

- Example: Emily diversifies her investment portfolio by allocating assets across stocks, bonds, real estate, and alternative investments to minimize risk and optimize returns.

2. Asset Allocation: Allocating investments based on risk tolerance, investment objectives, and time horizon to achieve a balanced portfolio that aligns with financial goals and risk management preferences.

   - Example: John rebalances his investment portfolio annually to maintain target asset allocation percentages and adjust investment positions based on market conditions and economic outlook.

3. Risk Assessment: Conducting periodic risk assessments, portfolio reviews, and stress tests to evaluate investment performance, identify potential risks, and make informed decisions.

   - Example: Sarah consults with a financial advisor to assess her risk tolerance, review investment strategies, and implement risk management measures to protect her retirement savings.

4. Insurance and Hedging: Utilizing insurance policies, options, futures contracts, or hedging strategies to mitigate specific investment risks, such as market volatility, currency fluctuations, or commodity price movements.

   - Example: Mark purchases put options to hedge against potential downside risk in his stock portfolio during market corrections or economic uncertainties.

An extensive exploration of investment strategies, emphasizing the power of compounding, opportunities in real estate and property investments, insights into stocks and other investment vehicles, and effective risk management technique is essential in wealth building. By understanding these principles and implementing sound investment strategies, individuals can optimize returns, protect their investments, and achieve long-term financial goals. The next chapters will delve into advanced investment techniques.

Chapter 5:

Weeding and Pruning: Overcoming Obstacles

Building wealth involves navigating various challenges, setbacks, and risks that can impact financial stability and success. This chapter explores strategies and insights to overcome obstacles in wealth building, including debt management, handling financial setbacks, avoiding scams and frauds, and leveraging emotional intelligence for sustainable financial growth.

Debt Management: Strategies for Paying Off Debt and Staying Debt-Free

Effective debt management is crucial for achieving financial independence, reducing financial stress, and maintaining a healthy credit profile. By adopting disciplined strategies and practices, individuals can pay off debt systematically and avoid falling into debt traps.

Understanding Debt

1. Types of Debt: Differentiate between good debt, such as mortgage loans and student loans that enable asset acquisition or education, and bad debt, such as high-interest credit card debt or payday loans that incur excessive interest charges.

 - Example: Sarah uses a mortgage loan to purchase a home, benefiting from tax deductions on mortgage interest payments and property appreciation over time.

2. Debt Repayment Strategies: Implement debt repayment strategies, such as the debt snowball method (paying off smallest debts first) or the debt avalanche method (paying off highest-interest debts first), to reduce outstanding balances and interest costs.

 - Example: John prioritizes paying off high-interest credit card debt by allocating additional funds toward monthly payments and reducing outstanding balances to zero.

3. Budgeting and Financial Planning: Develop a budget, prioritize debt repayment within monthly expenses, and allocate surplus income toward paying off debts faster to achieve financial freedom.

  - Example: Emily creates a monthly budget that includes debt payments, living expenses, and savings goals, allocating a portion of her income to accelerate debt repayment and achieve financial goals.

4. Negotiating Debt Settlements: Negotiate with creditors or lenders to settle debts, negotiate lower interest rates, or consolidate multiple debts into a single loan with favorable terms and conditions.

  - Example: Mark negotiates a debt settlement agreement with creditors, agreeing to pay a reduced amount to settle outstanding debts and improve his financial standing.

Overcoming Financial Setbacks: How to Handle Economic Downturns, Job Loss, or Failed Investments

Financial setbacks, such as economic downturns, job loss, or failed investments, can disrupt financial stability and long-term wealth-building goals. Adopting resilience, proactive planning, and effective coping strategies is essential to navigate and overcome financial challenges.

Navigating Economic Downturns

1. Emergency Fund: Establish an emergency fund with three to six months' worth of living expenses to cover unexpected financial emergencies, job loss, or temporary income disruptions.

  - Example: Lisa maintains an emergency fund equivalent to six months of living expenses in a high-yield savings account, providing financial security during economic uncertainties.

2. Job Loss Preparedness: Develop job loss preparedness strategies, such as updating resumes, networking with industry contacts, and acquiring new skills or certifications to enhance employability.

  - Example: Mike attends professional development workshops and online courses to expand his skill set and stay competitive in the job market during economic downturns.

3. Diversified Investments: Diversify investment portfolios across different asset classes, industries, and geographic regions to mitigate investment risk and reduce vulnerability to market volatility.

  - Example: Emma diversifies her investment portfolio by allocating assets across stocks, bonds, real estate, and alternative investments, minimizing the impact of market downturns on overall portfolio performance.

4. Financial Contingency Planning: Develop contingency plans and alternative income sources, such as freelancing, consulting, or part-time work, to supplement income and maintain financial stability during economic downturns.

  - Example: Jack explores freelance opportunities in graphic design and digital marketing to generate additional income and offset financial losses during economic downturns.

Avoiding Scams and Frauds: Recognizing and Avoiding Financial Pitfalls

Financial scams and frauds pose significant risks to individuals' financial well-being, integrity, and trust. Recognizing common scams, exercising caution, and implementing preventive measures can safeguard personal finances and investments from fraudulent activities.

Types of Financial Scams

1. Investment Scams: Identify red flags of investment scams, such as guaranteed high returns, unsolicited investment offers, and pressure to make immediate investment decisions without thorough due diligence.

   - Example: Sarah conducts thorough research, reviews investment prospectuses, and consults with financial advisors before making investment decisions to avoid fraudulent schemes.

2. Phishing and Identity Theft: Protect personal information, passwords, and financial credentials from phishing attacks, fraudulent emails, and online scams targeting sensitive data.

   - Example: John verifies website security features, uses secure passwords, and enables two-factor authentication to prevent unauthorized access to financial accounts and personal information.

3. Ponzi Schemes and Pyramid Schemes: Beware of Ponzi schemes promising high returns based on new investor contributions rather than legitimate business activities or investments.

   - Example: Emily conducts background checks on investment promoters, verifies business registrations, and avoids participating in Ponzi schemes offering unsustainable returns.

4. Advance Fee Scams: Exercise caution with advance fee scams requiring upfront payments or fees to access promised rewards, prizes, or financial opportunities.

   - Example: Mark ignores unsolicited emails, phone calls, or messages requesting advance payments or personal financial information to prevent falling victim to advance fee scams.

Emotional Intelligence in Wealth Building: Managing Emotions That Can Derail Financial Plans

Emotional intelligence plays a critical role in making rational financial decisions, managing financial behaviors, and achieving long-term wealth-building success. Developing self-awareness, emotional regulation, and financial resilience enhances decision-making capabilities and promotes financial well-being.

Emotional Challenges in Wealth Building

1. Fear and Anxiety: Recognize and manage fear and anxiety related to financial uncertainty, market volatility, or investment decisions to avoid impulsive behaviors or irrational financial choices.

  - Example: Lisa practices mindfulness techniques, such as deep breathing exercises and meditation, to reduce stress levels and maintain emotional balance during financial challenges.

2. Greed and Overconfidence: Avoid succumbing to greed or overconfidence in investment opportunities, speculative ventures, or get-rich-quick schemes that carry high risks and potential losses.

  - Example: Mike consults with financial advisors, sets realistic investment goals, and adheres to disciplined investment strategies to mitigate risks associated with greed and overconfidence.

3. Impulse Buying and Lifestyle Inflation: Resist impulse buying, unnecessary expenses, or lifestyle inflation that can deplete savings, hinder debt repayment, and undermine long-term financial goals.

- Example: Emma creates a spending plan, tracks expenses, and prioritizes savings goals to resist impulse purchases and maintain financial discipline in achieving wealth-building objectives.

4. Patience and Delayed Gratification: Cultivate patience, delayed gratification, and long-term perspective in wealth-building strategies, investment decisions, and financial planning processes.

  - Example: Jack sets long-term investment goals, establishes investment timelines, and adheres to disciplined savings habits to achieve financial milestones and long-term wealth accumulation.

One could walk in lights of sound financial decision- making by employing these strategies for overcoming obstacles in wealth building, including effective debt management, navigating financial setbacks, recognizing and avoiding scams and frauds, and leveraging emotional intelligence for sound financial decision-making. By implementing proactive strategies, exercising caution, and cultivating financial resilience, individuals can protect their financial well-being, achieve financial goals, and navigate challenges on the path to long-term financial success. The next chapters will delve into advanced financial planning strategies, retirement planning, and legacy wealth management to further empower readers in their financial journey.

Chapter 6:

Harvesting Wealth: Realizing Financial Goals

Achieving financial goals and harvesting wealth involves strategic planning, disciplined execution, and mindful decision-making to sustain long-term prosperity. This chapter explores key principles, strategies, and insights to empower individuals in realizing financial aspirations, cultivating financial well-being, and contributing positively to society through philanthropy.

Setting and Achieving Milestones: Breaking Down Long-Term Financial Goals into Achievable Steps

Setting clear, measurable milestones is essential for navigating the path to financial success, maintaining motivation, and tracking progress toward achieving long-term financial goals.

Establishing Financial Goals

1. Short-term, Mid-term, and Long-term Goals: Differentiate between short-term goals (e.g., building an emergency fund), mid-term goals (e.g., purchasing a home), and long-term goals (e.g., retirement savings) to prioritize financial objectives and allocate resources effectively.

   - Example: Sarah prioritizes short-term goals, such as paying off credit card debt, mid-term goals, such as saving for a down payment on a home, and long-term goals, such as funding retirement accounts, to achieve financial milestones systematically.

2. SMART Goals: Create SMART (Specific, Measurable, Achievable, Relevant, Time-bound) goals to clarify objectives, define actionable steps, and monitor progress toward achieving financial milestones.

- Example: John sets a SMART goal to increase monthly savings contributions by 10% over the next year, track progress monthly, and adjust budgeting strategies to achieve savings goals effectively.

3. Financial Planning Tools: Utilize financial planning tools, such as budgeting apps, retirement calculators, and investment trackers, to evaluate financial health, project future outcomes, and optimize financial decisions aligned with personal goals.

- Example: Emily uses a retirement calculator to estimate future retirement income needs, assess investment strategies, and adjust retirement savings contributions to achieve targeted financial milestones by retirement age.

The Art of Saving and Spending Wisely: Finding a Balance Between Enjoying Wealth and Sustaining It

Achieving financial balance involves cultivating prudent saving habits, adopting mindful spending practices, and striking a harmonious equilibrium between enjoying present-day comforts and securing future financial security.

Principles of Saving and Spending

1. Budgeting and Expense Management: Develop a comprehensive budget, track expenses diligently, and prioritize essential needs over discretionary spending to optimize financial resources and achieve savings goals effectively.

- Example: Lisa allocates fixed percentages of income to essential expenses (e.g., housing, utilities), variable expenses (e.g., groceries, entertainment), and savings goals (e.g., retirement contributions, emergency fund) within her monthly budget.

2. Emergency Fund: Establish and maintain an emergency fund with sufficient savings equivalent to three to six months' worth of living expenses to prepare for unexpected financial emergencies, job loss, or medical expenses.

- Example: Mike accumulates savings in a high-yield savings account dedicated to emergency funds, ensuring financial resilience and peace of mind during unforeseen circumstances.

3. Investing in Future Goals: Prioritize long-term financial goals, such as retirement savings, education funds for children, or personal investments, by allocating a portion of income to investment accounts and wealth-building strategies.

   - Example: Jack contributes regularly to retirement accounts, monitors investment performance, and adjusts asset allocation strategies to maximize long-term investment returns and achieve retirement goals.

Wealth vs. Riches: Understanding the Difference and Why It Matters

Differentiate between wealth and riches, emphasizing sustainable wealth accumulation, financial independence, and holistic well-being over material possessions or temporary financial gains.

Defining Wealth and Riches

1. Wealth: Wealth encompasses accumulated assets, financial resources, and investments generating passive income, providing financial security, and supporting long-term lifestyle goals and aspirations.

   - Example: Emma prioritizes wealth accumulation through diversified investments, real estate properties, and retirement savings to achieve financial independence and sustain long-term prosperity.

2. Riches: Riches refer to temporary wealth, material possessions, or monetary gains often associated with high income, extravagant spending, or short-term financial success without sustainable wealth-building strategies.

- Example: Sarah distinguishes between riches acquired from a lottery win and sustainable wealth accumulated through disciplined saving, prudent investing, and financial planning strategies.

3. Sustainable Wealth-Building Practices: Adopt sustainable wealth-building practices, such as asset diversification, passive income streams, and long-term investment strategies, to achieve lasting financial security and lifestyle sustainability.

- Example: Mark invests in income-generating assets, such as dividend-paying stocks, rental properties, and business ventures, to build sustainable wealth and achieve financial freedom over time.

Philanthropy and Giving Back: The Role of Generosity in a Prosperous Life

Integrating philanthropy and charitable giving into financial planning fosters a sense of purpose, social responsibility, and community impact, enhancing personal fulfillment and contributing positively to society.

Benefits of Philanthropy

1. Social Impact: Support charitable organizations, community initiatives, or global causes aligned with personal values, social concerns, and humanitarian efforts to make a meaningful difference in society.

- Example: Lisa volunteers time and financial resources to local charities, participates in community outreach programs, and advocates for social causes to promote positive social change and improve quality of life.

2. Legacy and Impact Investing: Establish a philanthropic legacy through impact investing, charitable trusts, or donor-advised funds to support educational, environmental, or healthcare initiatives benefiting future generations.

- Example: Mike allocates a percentage of investment returns to impact investments, supporting sustainable development projects, and promoting environmental conservation efforts aligned with personal philanthropic goals.

3. Personal Fulfillment: Experience personal fulfillment, emotional satisfaction, and spiritual enrichment by contributing to philanthropic causes, fostering community engagement, and promoting societal well-being through generous acts of giving.

- Example: Emily incorporates charitable giving into financial planning, donates to humanitarian organizations, and participates in volunteer activities to create a positive impact and inspire others to embrace philanthropy.

In realizing your financial goals, you must employ these strategies for harvesting wealth through setting achievable financial milestones, embracing prudent saving and spending habits, understanding the difference between wealth and riches, and integrating philanthropy into financial planning. By adopting disciplined financial practices, maintaining long-term perspective, and prioritizing holistic well-being, individuals can achieve financial independence, sustain wealth accumulation, and contribute positively to society through philanthropic endeavors. The next chapters will delve into advanced wealth management strategies, legacy planning, and navigating financial transitions to empower readers in their journey toward enduring financial success and personal fulfillment.

Chapter 7:

Sustaining the Harvest: Wealth Preservation

Wealth preservation is crucial for maintaining financial stability, securing future generations, and ensuring sustainable growth of assets. This chapter explores essential strategies and principles to effectively preserve wealth, including inheritance planning, asset protection, tax management, and smart reinvestment strategies.

Inheritance and Legacy Planning: Ensuring Wealth Benefits Future Generations

Inheritance and legacy planning involve strategic decisions and legal arrangements to transfer assets, preserve wealth, and leave a lasting legacy for future generations.

Key Elements of Legacy Planning

1. Estate Planning: Develop a comprehensive estate plan, including wills, trusts, and powers of attorney, to specify asset distribution, designate beneficiaries, and minimize estate taxes upon death.

   - Example: Sarah consults with estate planning attorneys to draft a will, establish a revocable living trust, and designate beneficiaries to ensure orderly asset distribution and protect family wealth.

2. Multigenerational Wealth Transfer: Implement multigenerational wealth transfer strategies, such as family trusts or dynasty trusts, to pass assets to successive generations while minimizing tax implications and preserving family values.

   - Example: John establishes a dynasty trust to transfer assets to grandchildren, provide financial support for future generations, and maintain family wealth over multiple lifetimes.

3. Charitable Giving: Incorporate charitable giving strategies, such as donor-advised funds or charitable trusts, to support philanthropic causes, receive tax benefits, and leave a positive impact on communities.

   - Example: Emily establishes a donor-advised fund to support educational scholarships, environmental conservation projects, and healthcare initiatives, contributing to charitable organizations and leaving a philanthropic legacy.

Insurance and Protection: Safeguarding Assets Through Comprehensive Coverage

Insurance plays a pivotal role in asset protection by mitigating financial risks, providing security against unforeseen events, and safeguarding wealth accumulation from potential liabilities.

Types of Insurance Coverage

1. Life Insurance: Purchase life insurance policies, such as term life or whole life insurance, to provide financial security, replace income, and support dependents in the event of premature death.

   - Example: Mike obtains a term life insurance policy with coverage equivalent to ten times his annual income, ensuring financial protection for his family and covering mortgage obligations in case of unexpected death.

2. Property and Casualty Insurance: Obtain property insurance, including homeowner's insurance or renter's insurance, to protect real estate properties, personal belongings, and mitigate financial losses from natural disasters or property damage.

   - Example: Emma secures homeowner's insurance coverage for her primary residence, covering property damages, liability claims, and personal belongings against unforeseen risks and natural disasters.

3. Liability Insurance: Acquire liability insurance, such as umbrella insurance policies, to extend liability coverage beyond standard limits, protect assets from lawsuits, and mitigate financial risks associated with legal claims or personal injury lawsuits.

  - Example: Jack purchases umbrella insurance coverage to supplement existing liability limits, protect personal assets from potential lawsuits, and ensure comprehensive financial protection against unforeseen liabilities.

The Role of Taxes in Wealth Preservation: Understanding Tax Obligations and Minimizing Tax Burdens

Effective tax planning strategies are essential for minimizing tax liabilities, optimizing financial resources, and preserving wealth accumulation through proactive tax management and compliance.

Tax Planning Strategies

1. Income Tax Management: Implement income tax planning strategies, such as maximizing tax deductions, contributing to tax-advantaged retirement accounts (e.g., 401(k) plans, IRAs), and leveraging tax credits to reduce taxable income and lower overall tax liabilities.

  - Example: Lisa contributes to a traditional IRA, benefiting from tax-deferred growth, reducing taxable income, and optimizing retirement savings while minimizing current income tax obligations.

2. Estate Tax Mitigation: Utilize estate planning tools, such as marital deductions, charitable bequests, and lifetime gifting strategies, to minimize estate taxes, preserve family wealth, and facilitate tax-efficient wealth transfer to heirs.

- Example: Sarah employs annual gift exclusions to transfer assets tax-free to beneficiaries, reducing taxable estate values and maximizing wealth preservation through strategic estate planning techniques.

3. Capital Gains Tax Strategies: Implement capital gains tax planning strategies, such as tax-loss harvesting, holding assets for long-term capital gains rates, and utilizing tax-deferred investment accounts to minimize tax implications on investment gains and maximize after-tax returns.

- Example: Mark employs tax-loss harvesting techniques to offset capital gains with capital losses, reduce taxable investment income, and optimize portfolio performance while adhering to tax-efficient investment strategies.

Continuous Reinvestment: Keeping Wealth Growing Through Smart Reinvestment Strategies

Continuous reinvestment strategies are essential for maintaining wealth growth, enhancing investment returns, and optimizing financial resources through disciplined reinvestment of dividends, interest income, and capital gains.

Principles of Reinvestment

1. Dividend Reinvestment Plans (DRIPs): Participate in dividend reinvestment plans offered by companies or mutual funds to reinvest dividends automatically, accumulate additional shares, and compound investment returns over time.

- Example: Emily enrolls in a DRIP program, reinvesting dividends earned from stock investments to purchase additional shares, capitalize on compound growth, and maximize long-term investment returns.

2. Portfolio Rebalancing: Conduct periodic portfolio rebalancing by adjusting asset allocations, reallocating investments among different asset classes, and maintaining strategic diversification to optimize risk-adjusted returns and adapt to changing market conditions.

- Example: Mike reviews portfolio performance, rebalances asset allocations periodically, and reallocates investments based on financial goals, risk tolerance, and market outlook to achieve optimal investment outcomes.

3. Tax-Efficient Investments: Invest in tax-efficient investment vehicles, such as municipal bonds, index funds, or tax-managed mutual funds, to minimize taxable investment income, reduce tax liabilities, and preserve after-tax investment returns.

- Example: Emma diversifies investment holdings across tax-exempt municipal bonds, tax-advantaged retirement accounts, and low-cost index funds, optimizing portfolio tax efficiency and preserving wealth through prudent investment strategies.

Applying these strategies for financial sustainability will establish the harvest through wealth preservation, including inheritance and legacy planning, insurance and asset protection, tax management, and continuous reinvestment strategies. By implementing comprehensive wealth preservation strategies, managing financial risks effectively, and optimizing tax efficiency, individuals can safeguard accumulated wealth, support future generations, and achieve long-term financial security and prosperity. The next chapters will delve into advanced wealth management techniques, philanthropic initiatives, and preparing for financial transitions to empower readers in navigating complex financial landscapes and achieving enduring financial success.

Chapter 8:

The Farmer's Toolbox: Essential Skills for Wealth Creation

Wealth creation requires more than financial acumen; it demands a diverse set of skills to navigate challenges, seize opportunities, and sustain long-term success. This chapter explores essential skills that serve as foundational tools for individuals striving to cultivate and grow wealth in a dynamic economic environment.

Time Management and Productivity: Maximizing Time as a Crucial Resource

Effective time management and productivity are critical for optimizing efficiency, accomplishing goals, and leveraging time as a valuable asset in wealth creation endeavors.

Principles of Time Management

1. Goal Setting and Prioritization: Set clear, actionable goals, prioritize tasks based on urgency and importance, and allocate time effectively to maximize productivity and achieve desired outcomes.

  - Example: Sarah sets daily, weekly, and monthly goals, uses task prioritization techniques (e.g., Eisenhower Matrix), and schedules focused work sessions to optimize time management and enhance productivity in achieving financial milestones.

2. Time Blocking and Scheduling: Implement time blocking techniques, create structured schedules, and allocate dedicated time slots for specific tasks, projects, or activities to minimize distractions and maintain focus on high-priority tasks.

  - Example: John adopts time blocking methods, schedules uninterrupted work periods for completing financial analyses or investment research, and adheres to predetermined time allocations to enhance productivity and meet deadlines effectively.

3. **Eliminating Time Wasters:** Identify and eliminate time-wasting activities, distractions, or inefficiencies, such as excessive social media use, unnecessary meetings, or procrastination habits, to optimize time utilization and increase productivity levels.

   - Example: Emily limits social media usage during work hours, delegates non-essential tasks to team members, and implements time management tools (e.g., Pomodoro Technique) to minimize distractions and enhance concentration on wealth creation activities.

Networking and Relationships: Building and Leveraging Connections for Wealth Creation

Networking and cultivating meaningful relationships play a pivotal role in expanding opportunities, gaining valuable insights, and accessing resources essential for wealth creation and professional growth.

Strategies for Effective Networking

1. Building a Professional Network: Actively engage in networking events, industry conferences, and professional associations to connect with peers, mentors, industry experts, and potential collaborators who can offer valuable guidance, support, and opportunities.

   - Example: Mike attends networking events hosted by financial industry associations, participates in professional development workshops, and cultivates relationships with industry professionals to expand his professional network and access career advancement opportunities.

2. **Maintaining Relationships:** Nurture and maintain meaningful relationships with contacts, mentors, and business partners through regular communication, follow-ups,

and mutual support to establish trust, credibility, and long-term collaborative partnerships.

- Example: Emma maintains regular communication with industry contacts, schedules periodic meetings or virtual coffee chats, and offers assistance or valuable insights to foster strong professional relationships and leverage networking opportunities for career advancement and wealth creation endeavors.

3. Utilizing Digital Networking Platforms: Leverage digital networking platforms, such as LinkedIn or industry-specific forums, to expand professional networks, share expertise, and engage in thought leadership activities to enhance visibility, credibility, and networking effectiveness.

- Example: Jack maintains an updated LinkedIn profile, participates in industry discussions, shares relevant content or industry insights, and connects with like-minded professionals to expand his digital network and access new career opportunities or potential business ventures.

Negotiation and Communication Skills: Essential for Securing Deals and Opportunities

Effective negotiation and communication skills are essential for navigating business transactions, securing favorable deals, and capitalizing on opportunities critical to wealth creation and financial success.

Key Elements of Negotiation Skills

1. Preparation and Research: Conduct thorough research, gather relevant information, and prepare negotiation strategies, including setting goals, identifying interests, and understanding potential outcomes to negotiate effectively and achieve desired objectives.

- Example: Lisa conducts market research, analyzes comparable property sales data, and prepares negotiation strategies, such as offering competitive purchase offers or negotiating favorable terms and conditions to secure real estate investments and maximize investment returns.

2. Active Listening and Empathy: Practice active listening skills, demonstrate empathy, and seek to understand perspectives, concerns, or motivations of negotiation counterparts to build rapport, establish trust, and facilitate mutually beneficial agreements or partnerships.

- Example: Sarah listens attentively to client preferences, addresses concerns, and proposes customized financial solutions or investment strategies that align with client objectives, demonstrating empathy and building trust to secure long-term client relationships and enhance business growth.

3. Conflict Resolution: Apply conflict resolution techniques, such as seeking common ground, exploring alternative solutions, and maintaining professionalism, to manage conflicts, resolve disputes, and preserve positive relationships during negotiation processes.

- Example: John mediates disagreements between team members, facilitates open communication, and encourages collaborative problem-solving approaches to address conflicts, foster teamwork, and achieve collective goals effectively within financial organizations or investment firms.

Resilience and Adaptability: Thriving in a Constantly Changing Economic Landscape

Resilience and adaptability are essential attributes for navigating challenges, overcoming setbacks, and thriving in a dynamic economic environment characterized by uncertainties, market fluctuations, and evolving business trends.

JEFFREY BENSON

Strategies for Building Resilience

1. Embracing Change: Embrace change, stay informed about industry trends, economic developments, or technological advancements, and adapt strategies, business models, or investment approaches to capitalize on opportunities and mitigate risks effectively.

  - Example: Emily monitors market trends, evaluates emerging technologies, and adjusts investment portfolios or business strategies accordingly to capitalize on growth opportunities, optimize investment returns, and sustain long-term financial success in competitive markets.

2. Learning from Setbacks: Learn from setbacks, failures, or unexpected challenges, reflect on lessons learned, and leverage resilience to bounce back stronger, refine strategies, and pursue new opportunities with determination, perseverance, and a positive mindset.

  - Example: Mike analyzes investment losses, identifies factors contributing to setbacks, and adjusts risk management strategies, asset allocations, or investment decisions to mitigate future risks, enhance portfolio performance, and achieve investment goals effectively.

3. Seeking Support and Guidance: Seek support from mentors, advisors, or professional networks, discuss challenges or concerns, and leverage collective insights, experience, or expertise to navigate complexities, make informed decisions, and achieve professional or financial objectives effectively.

  - Example: Emma seeks guidance from industry mentors, consults with financial advisors, and participates in peer support groups or professional networks to receive feedback, gain valuable perspectives, and access resources necessary for overcoming challenges, making strategic decisions, and achieving career or wealth creation goals.

Understanding these essential skills for wealth creation, including time management, productivity, networking, negotiation, communication skills, resilience, and adaptability is key in your journey of cultivating wealth beyond riches. By developing and mastering these foundational skills, individuals can enhance productivity, expand professional networks, negotiate effectively, and navigate challenges or uncertainties in the pursuit of long-term financial success and prosperity. The next chapters will delve into advanced strategies for entrepreneurial success, leadership development, and strategic wealth management to empower readers in achieving their aspirations, advancing careers, and cultivating sustainable wealth creation in competitive global markets.

Chapter 9:

The Seasonal Cycles of Wealth

Understanding the seasonal cycles of wealth is crucial for navigating economic fluctuations, adapting strategies to market conditions, and preparing for both prosperous periods and economic downturns. This chapter explores key concepts, strategies, and insights to empower individuals in effectively managing wealth across different economic cycles.

Understanding Economic Cycles: Recognizing the Phases of Boom and Bust in the Economy

Economic cycles refer to the recurring patterns of expansion and contraction in economic activity, characterized by periods of growth (boom) and decline (bust), influenced by various factors such as business cycles, fiscal policies, and global economic trends.

Phases of Economic Cycles

1. Expansion (Boom): During the expansion phase, economic activity increases, characterized by rising GDP, consumer spending, business investments, and employment rates. Key indicators include robust market growth, increased consumer confidence, and expanding business opportunities.

   - Example: Sarah observes economic indicators, such as rising stock market indices, expanding job markets, and increased consumer expenditures on luxury goods or discretionary spending, signaling the onset of an economic expansion phase conducive to wealth creation and investment growth.

2. Peak: The peak marks the highest point of economic expansion, characterized by maximum GDP growth, peak business investments, and high consumer confidence levels. Key indicators include overheating markets, rising inflation rates, and potential signs of economic overheating or speculative bubbles.

- Example: John monitors economic indicators, such as overheated housing markets, rapid stock market gains, and excessive consumer borrowing, identifying peak economic conditions necessitating caution, risk management strategies, and portfolio diversification to mitigate potential risks and preserve wealth during economic peaks.

3. Contraction (Bust): During the contraction phase, economic activity declines, characterized by slowing GDP growth, reduced consumer spending, business retrenchments, and rising unemployment rates. Key indicators include declining stock market indices, shrinking business revenues, and increased financial uncertainties.

- Example: Emily recognizes economic indicators, such as declining consumer confidence, rising unemployment rates, and contracting business activities, signaling the onset of an economic contraction phase requiring defensive investment strategies, liquidity management, and financial resilience to navigate downturns and mitigate potential losses.

4. Trough: The trough represents the lowest point of economic contraction, characterized by minimal GDP growth, high unemployment rates, and depressed consumer spending. Key indicators include bottoming out of financial markets, economic stagnation, and widespread economic hardships.

- Example: Mike assesses economic indicators, such as stagnant business investments, persistently high unemployment rates, and sluggish economic recovery, identifying trough economic conditions necessitating strategic investment opportunities, long-term asset accumulation, and contrarian investment strategies to capitalize on undervalued assets and position for future economic recoveries.

Adjusting Strategies with Seasons: Adapting Wealth-Building Strategies to Economic Conditions

Adapting wealth-building strategies to economic conditions involves assessing market dynamics, identifying opportunities, and adjusting investment strategies, asset allocations, and financial decisions to optimize returns, manage risks, and achieve long-term financial objectives.

Strategic Adjustments Based on Economic Conditions

1. Expansionary Strategies: During economic expansions, adopt growth-oriented investment strategies, such as equity investments, venture capital, and real estate developments, to capitalize on rising asset valuations, business opportunities, and economic growth prospects.

 - Example: Lisa allocates investment portfolios to growth stocks, technology sectors, and emerging markets, leveraging economic expansions to maximize investment returns, diversify asset classes, and achieve long-term financial growth during favorable economic conditions.

2. Defensive Strategies: During economic contractions, implement defensive investment strategies, such as fixed-income securities, defensive stocks (e.g., utilities, consumer staples), and gold commodities, to preserve capital, mitigate downside risks, and safeguard investment portfolios from market volatility.

 - Example: Jack reallocates investment holdings to defensive sectors, bonds, and cash equivalents, reducing exposure to high-risk assets, minimizing potential losses, and maintaining liquidity during economic contractions to capitalize on safe-haven assets and protect wealth accumulation.

3. Diversification and Risk Management: Embrace diversified investment portfolios, asset allocations, and risk management strategies to balance risk-return profiles, mitigate portfolio volatility, and enhance resilience against economic uncertainties, market fluctuations, and geopolitical risks.

 - Example: Emma diversifies investment portfolios across asset classes, geographic regions, and industry sectors, implementing risk-adjusted strategies, and maintaining a balanced investment approach to optimize portfolio performance, mitigate concentration risks, and achieve sustainable wealth accumulation across economic cycles.

Reaping During the Harvest Season: Identifying the Right Time to Cash Out or Reinvest

Reaping during the harvest season involves strategically timing investment exits, profit-taking strategies, and reinvestment decisions based on market valuations, economic indicators, and financial goals to optimize investment returns and capitalize on market opportunities.

Strategic Timing for Investment Decisions

1. Profit-Taking Strategies: Identify optimal profit-taking opportunities, evaluate investment gains, and implement disciplined sell strategies to realize capital gains, rebalance portfolios, and lock in investment profits during bullish market conditions.

   - Example: Sarah monitors investment performance metrics, analyzes market trends, and executes profit-taking strategies by selling overvalued stocks, rebalancing portfolio allocations, and reallocating funds to undervalued assets or alternative investment opportunities to capitalize on investment gains and optimize portfolio returns.

2. Reinvestment Strategies: Reinvest investment proceeds into high-potential assets, growth-oriented sectors, or income-generating opportunities to maximize capital growth, compound investment returns, and sustain long-term wealth accumulation objectives.

   - Example: John reinvests capital gains into diversified investment portfolios, allocates funds to growth-oriented sectors (e.g., technology, healthcare), and leverages dollar-cost averaging techniques to enhance investment returns, capitalize on market opportunities, and achieve sustainable wealth growth during favorable market conditions.

JEFFREY BENSON

Preparing for the Winter: Building a Financial Cushion for Economic Downturns

Preparing for economic downturns involves establishing financial resilience, building emergency funds, implementing risk management strategies, and maintaining liquidity to navigate uncertainties, preserve wealth, and safeguard financial stability during challenging economic environments.

Strategies for Financial Preparedness

1. Emergency Fund: Establish and maintain emergency funds equivalent to three to six months' worth of living expenses to cover unforeseen financial emergencies, job loss, or unexpected medical expenses during economic downturns.

- Example: Emily accumulates savings in a dedicated emergency fund, maintains liquid assets, and implements cash flow management strategies to withstand economic uncertainties, mitigate financial risks, and ensure financial stability during downturns.

2. Debt Management: Reduce debt obligations, prioritize debt repayment strategies, and manage credit usage to minimize financial burdens, lower interest expenses, and enhance financial flexibility during economic contractions.

- Example: Mike adopts debt consolidation methods, prioritizes high-interest debt repayments, and maintains disciplined credit card usage to reduce debt liabilities, improve credit scores, and strengthen financial resilience against economic downturns.

3. Risk Mitigation and Insurance Coverage: Review insurance policies, assess coverage needs, and obtain adequate insurance protection, such as health insurance, disability insurance, and homeowners' insurance, to mitigate financial risks, protect assets, and ensure comprehensive risk management during economic uncertainties.

- Example: Jack evaluates insurance coverage options, updates policy beneficiaries, and secures comprehensive insurance protections, including life insurance, health insurance, and property insurance, to safeguard personal finances, mitigate potential losses, and preserve wealth accumulation during economic downturns.

Wealth building requires applying these strategies for walking in the lights of the seasonal cycles of wealth, including economic cycles, strategies adjustment, reaping during prosperous times, and preparing for economic downturns. By understanding economic dynamics, adapting wealth-building strategies, strategically timing investment decisions, and preparing for financial uncertainties, individuals can navigate economic fluctuations, optimize investment returns, and achieve sustainable wealth preservation across different economic cycles. The next chapters will delve into advanced investment strategies, global economic trends, and emerging opportunities to empower readers in navigating complex financial landscapes, making informed decisions, and achieving enduring financial success and prosperity.

Chapter 10:

The Wealth Farmer's Legacy

Building a legacy of wealth goes beyond financial prosperity; it encompasses ethical stewardship, intergenerational wealth transfer, and fostering a sustainable impact on society. This chapter explores strategies, principles, and ethical considerations essential for creating a lasting legacy of wealth and prosperity.

Building a Legacy of Wealth: Strategies for Ensuring Your Wealth Endures Through Generations

Creating a lasting legacy of wealth involves strategic planning, prudent financial management, and proactive measures to preserve, protect, and grow assets for future generations.

Key Strategies for Legacy Building

1. Estate Planning and Wealth Transfer: Develop comprehensive estate plans, establish trusts, and draft wills to facilitate smooth wealth transfer, minimize tax liabilities, and ensure assets are distributed according to your wishes.

   - Example: Sarah consults with estate planning attorneys, creates a testamentary trust, and outlines specific distribution instructions in her will to preserve family wealth, minimize probate costs, and safeguard financial legacies for future heirs and beneficiaries.

2. Family Governance Structures: Establish family offices, governance frameworks, or advisory boards to facilitate transparent communication, decision-making processes, and collaborative efforts among family members in managing shared assets and preserving family values.

- Example: John forms a family council, appoints family members to key roles, and implements governance policies, such as succession plans, conflict resolution mechanisms, and financial education programs to foster unity, trust, and continuity in preserving multi-generational wealth and achieving long-term financial objectives.

3. Philanthropic Initiatives: Allocate resources to philanthropic endeavors, charitable foundations, or community projects to create positive social impact, support meaningful causes, and leave a legacy of philanthropy that reflects personal values, beliefs, and commitments to societal well-being.

- Example: Emma establishes a charitable foundation, funds educational scholarships, and partners with nonprofit organizations to address social inequalities, promote environmental sustainability, and empower disadvantaged communities, leaving a philanthropic legacy that extends beyond financial wealth and enhances societal prosperity.

Teaching Financial Literacy to the Next Generation: Preparing Your Heirs to Manage and Grow Wealth

Educating future heirs about financial literacy, responsible stewardship, and wealth management principles is essential for preparing them to effectively manage inherited assets, make informed financial decisions, and sustain family legacies.

Strategies for Teaching Financial Literacy

1. Financial Education Programs: Implement structured financial education programs, workshops, or seminars to educate heirs about investment strategies, risk management techniques, and wealth preservation strategies tailored to their age, experience, and financial responsibilities.

- Example: Jack organizes financial literacy workshops, invites guest speakers, and introduces heirs to basic financial concepts, such as budgeting, saving, and investing, to equip them with essential knowledge and skills needed to make informed financial decisions, manage inherited assets responsibly, and preserve family legacies.

2. Hands-On Experience: Provide practical opportunities for heirs to gain hands-on experience in managing financial portfolios, making investment decisions, and participating in family wealth discussions to foster financial confidence, competence, and leadership skills.

   - Example: Lisa mentors heirs, involves them in investment discussions, and encourages them to manage designated investment portfolios to gain practical experience, develop critical thinking skills, and assume active roles in safeguarding and growing family wealth over successive generations.

3. Values-Based Education: Integrate values-based education, ethical considerations, and social responsibility into financial education initiatives to instill core values, principles of integrity, and ethical standards that guide heirs' financial behaviors, decision-making processes, and contributions to society.

   - Example: Mike incorporates ethical dilemmas, case studies, and ethical decision-making frameworks into financial literacy curricula, encourages heirs to reflect on moral implications of financial choices, and emphasizes the importance of integrity, honesty, and social responsibility in preserving family legacies and advancing philanthropic efforts.

Sustainable Wealth and Ethical Considerations: The Moral and Social Responsibilities of Wealth

Managing wealth ethically involves balancing financial success with moral obligations, social impact considerations, and sustainable practices that contribute to long-term prosperity for individuals, families, and communities.

JEFFREY BENSON

Ethical Considerations in Wealth Management

1. **Social Impact Investing:** Allocate capital to socially responsible investments, impact-driven initiatives, or sustainable development projects that promote environmental stewardship, social equity, and inclusive economic growth while generating positive financial returns.

   - Example: Emily invests in renewable energy projects, supports fair-trade enterprises, and advocates for corporate sustainability practices to align investment strategies with environmental conservation goals, social justice principles, and ethical standards that prioritize long-term sustainability and community well-being.

2. **Corporate Governance and Transparency:** Advocate for corporate governance reforms, transparency measures, and ethical business practices within investment portfolios, companies, or organizations to promote accountability, mitigate corporate risks, and enhance stakeholder trust in responsible wealth management practices.

   - Example: Emma serves on corporate boards, promotes governance best practices, and advocates for diversity, equity, and inclusion initiatives to strengthen corporate accountability, foster ethical leadership, and uphold transparency standards that align with ethical principles, social values, and sustainable business practices.

3. **Charitable Giving and Community Engagement:** Support charitable causes, volunteerism, or community outreach programs that address pressing societal needs, promote social justice, and empower marginalized populations to create positive social impact, advance philanthropic goals, and leave a legacy of compassion, generosity, and civic responsibility.

   - Example: Lisa volunteers at local charities, sponsors educational programs, and donates to humanitarian relief efforts to alleviate poverty, support educational opportunities, and empower underserved communities, demonstrating a commitment to ethical giving, social responsibility, and sustainable wealth stewardship that enriches lives and strengthens community bonds.

JEFFREY BENSON

Final Thoughts: The Wealth Farmer's Creed - Core Principles to Live By in the Pursuit of Lasting Prosperity

In conclusion, the Wealth Farmer's Creed encapsulates core principles, values, and guiding philosophies that inspire individuals to pursue lasting prosperity, uphold ethical standards, and leave a positive legacy that transcends financial wealth.

Core Principles of the Wealth Farmer's Creed

1. Integrity and Trustworthiness: Uphold principles of integrity, honesty, and transparency in all financial dealings, decisions, and interactions to build trust, foster credibility, and preserve ethical standards that define personal integrity and professional conduct.

2. Stewardship and Responsibility: Embrace stewardship responsibilities, demonstrate responsible financial management practices, and prioritize sustainability initiatives that safeguard natural resources, protect environmental ecosystems, and promote long-term prosperity for future generations.

3. Generosity and Philanthropy: Cultivate a spirit of generosity, compassion, and philanthropy by giving back to communities, supporting charitable causes, and advocating for social justice initiatives that empower individuals, promote equality, and create positive societal impact through acts of kindness, empathy, and humanitarianism.

4. Continual Learning and Growth: Commit to lifelong learning, professional development, and personal growth initiatives that enhance knowledge, expand skill sets, and foster innovation in wealth management practices, investment strategies, and entrepreneurial endeavors that lead to continuous improvement, adaptation, and sustainable success.

Building a legacy of wealth; requires applying the ethical considerations in wealth management, and the principles of the Wealth Farmer's Creed. By integrating ethical values, responsible stewardship, and sustainable practices into wealth management strategies, individuals can cultivate enduring legacies of prosperity, empower future generations to uphold ethical standards, and leave a positive impact on society that transcends financial wealth. The next chapters will delve into advanced topics in global finance, emerging market trends, and innovative strategies for achieving financial independence, advancing economic prosperity, and sustaining long-term wealth creation in a dynamic global economy.

Chapter 11:

Personal Stories of Harvesting Wealth

Personal stories of harvesting wealth are powerful narratives of individuals who have navigated challenges, embraced opportunities, and achieved financial success through perseverance, strategic thinking, and resilience. This chapter explores real-life examples, lessons learned, and stories of overcoming setbacks to inspire and empower readers in their own wealth-building journeys.

Success Stories: Real-Life Examples of Individuals Who Have Successfully Built and Sustained Wealth

Success stories showcase individuals from diverse backgrounds who have leveraged their skills, seized opportunities, and implemented effective strategies to build and sustain wealth over time.

Examples of Success

1. Sarah's Entrepreneurial Journey: Sarah, a tech entrepreneur, founded a startup in artificial intelligence (AI) solutions. Through strategic partnerships, innovative product development, and effective market positioning, Sarah grew her company into a market leader, generating substantial revenue and achieving a successful exit through acquisition.

  - **Key Strategies:** Sarah emphasized product innovation, customer-centric strategies, and scalability to capitalize on emerging market trends, attract venture capital investments, and achieve exponential growth in the competitive tech industry.

  - Lessons Learned: Sarah's success underscores the importance of innovation, resilience in overcoming challenges, and strategic vision in scaling business operations, driving market expansion, and achieving sustainable wealth creation through entrepreneurial ventures.

2. John's Investment Portfolio: John, a financial analyst, diversified his investment portfolio across asset classes, including stocks, bonds, and real estate properties. By adopting a disciplined investment approach, conducting thorough research, and leveraging market insights, John generated consistent returns, preserved capital, and achieved financial independence.

  - Key Strategies: John prioritized asset diversification, risk management, and long-term investment planning to optimize portfolio performance, mitigate market volatility, and capitalize on investment opportunities that aligned with his financial goals and risk tolerance.

  - Lessons Learned: John's success highlights the significance of diversification, disciplined investment practices, and informed decision-making in navigating financial markets, maximizing investment returns, and achieving sustainable wealth accumulation over the long term.

3. Emma's Philanthropic Impact: Emma, a social entrepreneur, founded a nonprofit organization dedicated to promoting environmental sustainability and community development initiatives. Through strategic partnerships, fundraising campaigns, and advocacy efforts, Emma mobilized resources, raised awareness, and empowered communities to address pressing social and environmental challenges.

  - Key Strategies: Emma prioritized social impact investing, sustainable development goals, and corporate social responsibility initiatives to foster positive change, advance environmental conservation efforts, and create meaningful social impact that enhances quality of life and promotes sustainable development.

  - Lessons Learned: Emma's philanthropic journey underscores the importance of social responsibility, ethical leadership, and community engagement in driving sustainable development, promoting social equity, and leaving a legacy of compassion, generosity, and positive societal impact through philanthropic endeavors.

Lessons Learned: What These Stories Teach Us About Perseverance, Strategy, and Mindset

Personal stories of harvesting wealth provide valuable insights into the principles, strategies, and mindset required to achieve financial success and overcome challenges along the way.

Key Lessons

1. Perseverance and Resilience: Success often requires perseverance, resilience, and determination to overcome obstacles, adapt to changing circumstances, and persist in pursuing long-term goals despite setbacks or failures.

  - Example: Jack's entrepreneurial journey illustrates the importance of perseverance, resilience, and tenacity in navigating business challenges, overcoming setbacks, and achieving sustainable growth and success in competitive industries.

2. Strategic Thinking and Planning: Effective wealth management involves strategic thinking, proactive planning, and disciplined execution of investment strategies, business ventures, and financial decisions to maximize opportunities, mitigate risks, and achieve long-term financial goals.

  - Example: Lisa's investment success demonstrates the significance of strategic thinking, thorough research, and informed decision-making in optimizing investment returns, managing portfolio risks, and capitalizing on market opportunities that align with financial objectives and risk tolerance levels.

3. Mindset and Growth Orientation: Adopting a growth mindset, embracing continuous learning, and seeking personal development opportunities are essential for fostering innovation, adapting to industry trends, and expanding skill sets that enhance professional growth and career advancement.

- Example: Mike's career achievements highlight the importance of mindset, continuous learning, and professional development in overcoming challenges, seizing career opportunities, and achieving personal success in dynamic and competitive business environments.

Failures and Comebacks: Stories of Those Who Faced Setbacks But Eventually Found Success

Failure is often a stepping stone to success, as individuals learn from setbacks, adapt strategies, and persevere in pursuing their goals despite initial challenges or adversities.

Stories of Resilience and Comeback

1. Emily's Entrepreneurial Resilience: Emily launched a startup in the fashion industry but faced initial setbacks, including market competition, supply chain disruptions, and economic downturns. Through resilience, innovation, and strategic pivoting, Emily diversified product offerings, expanded market reach, and revitalized business operations to achieve sustainable growth and profitability.

- **Key Strategies:** Emily prioritized market research, customer feedback, and agile business strategies to identify emerging trends, capitalize on consumer preferences, and pivot business models that align with evolving market demands and industry dynamics.

- **Lessons Learned:** Emily's entrepreneurial journey exemplifies the importance of resilience, adaptability, and strategic pivoting in navigating business challenges, overcoming setbacks, and achieving entrepreneurial success through innovation, perseverance, and determination.

2. Mike's Career Reinvention: Mike experienced job loss during economic downturns but leveraged career setbacks as opportunities for professional reinvention, skill enhancement, and career transition into emerging industries. Through resilience, networking, and continuous learning, Mike diversified skill sets, pursued new career opportunities, and achieved career success in dynamic and competitive job markets.

- **Key Strategies:** Mike embraced career transitions, expanded professional networks, and pursued educational opportunities to enhance skill sets, build industry expertise, and adapt to evolving job market trends that support career growth, advancement, and professional success.

- **Lessons Learned**: Mike's career resilience underscores the importance of adaptability, lifelong learning, and proactive career management in navigating job transitions, overcoming setbacks, and achieving career success through resilience, perseverance, and determination.

Personal stories of harvesting wealth, including success stories, lessons learned, and stories of resilience and comeback will help you in cultivating wealth beyond riches. By examining real-life examples of individuals who have navigated challenges, seized opportunities, and achieved financial success through perseverance, strategic thinking, and resilience, readers gain valuable insights, inspiration, and practical strategies to apply in their own wealth-building journeys. The next chapters will delve into advanced topics in global finance, emerging market trends, and innovative strategies for achieving financial independence, advancing economic prosperity, and sustaining long-term wealth creation in a dynamic global economy.

Chapter 12:

Your Path to Prosperity

In this final chapter, we explore the essential elements of building your path to prosperity, encompassing the creation of a wealth blueprint, the importance of commitment and discipline, strategies for reviewing and adjusting your plan, and the holistic embrace of abundance in all facets of life.

Creating Your Wealth Blueprint: A Step-by-Step Guide to Building Your Personalized Wealth Plan

Creating a personalized wealth blueprint involves setting clear financial goals, developing actionable strategies, and implementing effective tactics to achieve long-term prosperity and financial independence.

Steps to Build Your Wealth Blueprint

1. Define Your Financial Goals: Identify short-term and long-term financial objectives, such as retirement planning, wealth accumulation, debt reduction, and lifestyle aspirations, to establish clear benchmarks and milestones for measuring progress and success.

   - Example: Sarah sets specific financial goals, including saving for retirement, investing in real estate properties, and funding her children's education, to prioritize financial planning, allocate resources effectively, and achieve personal and professional aspirations through strategic wealth management strategies.

2. Assess Your Current Financial Situation: Conduct a comprehensive financial assessment to evaluate income sources, assets, liabilities, expenses, and cash flow patterns, to gain a holistic understanding of your financial position and identify areas for improvement or optimization.

- Example: John analyzes his financial statements, reviews investment portfolios, and assesses income sources to identify potential opportunities for diversification, risk management, and asset allocation that align with financial goals, risk tolerance levels, and long-term wealth accumulation objectives.

3. Develop a Strategic Wealth Plan: Create a strategic wealth plan that outlines actionable steps, timelines, and resource allocation strategies to achieve financial objectives, maximize investment returns, mitigate risks, and optimize financial resources for sustainable wealth accumulation and long-term financial success.

- Example: Lisa designs a personalized wealth plan, integrates investment strategies, and implements asset allocation models to diversify investment portfolios, minimize portfolio risks, and achieve financial independence through strategic planning, disciplined execution, and proactive management.

4. Implement Financial Strategies: Execute financial strategies, monitor progress, and adjust tactics to adapt to changing market conditions, economic trends, and personal financial circumstances that support wealth-building objectives, optimize investment performance, and achieve long-term financial goals.

- Example: Mike implements investment strategies, manages portfolio risks, and adjusts asset allocations to capitalize on market opportunities, maximize investment returns, and achieve financial independence through disciplined planning, proactive decision-making, and strategic wealth management strategies.

Commitment and Discipline: The Importance of Staying the Course

Commitment and discipline are crucial in maintaining focus, adhering to financial goals, and overcoming challenges or setbacks encountered during the wealth-building journey.

JEFFREY BENSON

Key Principles of Commitment and Discipline

1. Set Clear Objectives: Define specific financial goals, establish achievable benchmarks, and prioritize tasks to maintain focus, track progress, and stay motivated in pursuing long-term financial objectives through commitment, dedication, and perseverance.

   - Example: Emily sets clear financial goals, outlines actionable steps, and prioritizes tasks to achieve wealth-building objectives, maintain financial discipline, and sustain momentum in pursuing personal and professional aspirations through strategic planning, disciplined execution, and proactive management.

2. Adopt Consistent Habits: Cultivate consistent habits, routines, and practices that support financial goals, promote responsible financial behaviors, and reinforce positive habits that contribute to long-term success, resilience, and personal growth in achieving financial independence.

   - Example: Emma develops consistent habits, implements financial routines, and practices responsible spending habits to achieve financial goals, manage expenses, and sustain progress in pursuing personal and professional aspirations through disciplined planning, proactive decision-making, and strategic wealth management strategies.

3. Monitor Progress Regularly: Track financial progress, review performance metrics, and assess outcomes to identify areas for improvement, refine strategies, and adapt tactics that align with changing market conditions, economic trends, and personal financial circumstances to achieve long-term financial success.

   - Example: Jack monitors financial progress, evaluates investment performance, and adjusts asset allocations to optimize portfolio returns, minimize risks, and achieve financial independence through disciplined planning, proactive decision-making, and strategic wealth management strategies.

Reviewing and Adjusting the Plan: Regular Check-Ins and Flexibility in Your Wealth Strategy

Regularly reviewing and adjusting your wealth plan is essential to accommodate changing financial goals, market dynamics, and personal circumstances that impact long-term financial success and wealth accumulation.

Strategies for Reviewing and Adjusting Your Wealth Plan

1. Conduct Periodic Assessments: Schedule regular financial check-ins, conduct comprehensive assessments, and evaluate progress toward financial goals to identify areas for improvement, refine strategies, and adjust tactics that support long-term wealth accumulation and financial independence.

   - Example: Sarah conducts periodic assessments, reviews investment portfolios, and evaluates financial strategies to optimize asset allocations, maximize investment returns, and achieve personal and professional aspirations through disciplined planning, proactive decision-making, and strategic wealth management strategies.

2. Monitor Market Trends: Stay informed about economic trends, industry developments, and market dynamics that impact investment performance, asset allocation strategies, and financial planning decisions to capitalize on opportunities, mitigate risks, and achieve long-term financial goals.

   - Example: John monitors market trends, evaluates economic indicators, and assesses investment opportunities to optimize asset allocations, diversify investment portfolios, and achieve financial independence through disciplined planning, proactive decision-making, and strategic wealth management strategies.

3. Adapt to Changing Circumstances: Adjust financial strategies, revise investment plans, and adapt asset allocation models to accommodate changing market conditions, economic trends, and personal financial circumstances that support long-term wealth accumulation, investment performance, and financial independence.

- Example: Lisa adapts financial strategies, revises investment plans, and adjusts asset allocation models to navigate market volatility, optimize investment returns, and achieve financial independence through disciplined planning, proactive decision-making, and strategic wealth management strategies.

Living a Life of Abundance: Embracing Prosperity in All Areas of Life, Not Just Financially

Living a life of abundance involves cultivating holistic well-being, fostering meaningful relationships, and pursuing personal fulfillment, happiness, and satisfaction beyond financial wealth and material possessions.

Components of Living a Life of Abundance

1. Prioritize Health and Wellness: Invest in physical health, mental well-being, and emotional resilience to enhance quality of life, promote longevity, and achieve holistic well-being that supports personal growth, professional success, and overall happiness.

   - Example: Mike prioritizes health and wellness, practices self-care routines, and fosters positive habits to maintain physical fitness, mental clarity, and emotional balance that contribute to holistic well-being, personal growth, and overall happiness through disciplined planning, proactive decision-making, and strategic wealth management strategies.

2. Cultivate Meaningful Relationships: Build and nurture meaningful relationships, foster social connections, and cultivate interpersonal bonds that promote mutual support, emotional intimacy, and social engagement to enhance personal happiness, satisfaction, and fulfillment in achieving life goals.

   - Example: Emma cultivates meaningful relationships, fosters social connections, and engages in community activities to build interpersonal bonds, strengthen social networks, and enhance personal happiness, satisfaction, and fulfillment in achieving life goals through disciplined planning, proactive decision-making, and strategic wealth management strategies.

3. Embrace Personal Fulfillment: Pursue passions, interests, and hobbies that ignite joy, creativity, and personal fulfillment to cultivate happiness, satisfaction, and emotional well-being that contribute to overall life satisfaction, positive mindset, and holistic well-being through disciplined planning, proactive decision-making, and strategic wealth management strategies.

- Example: Emily pursues passions, interests, and hobbies that ignite joy, creativity, and personal fulfillment to cultivate happiness, satisfaction, and emotional well-being that contribute to overall life satisfaction, positive mindset, and holistic well-being through disciplined planning, proactive decision-making, and strategic wealth management strategies.

These essential elements are vital for building your path to prosperity, including creating a wealth blueprint, committing to financial goals, reviewing and adjusting your plan in embracing abundance in all areas of life. By developing a personalized wealth plan, prioritizing commitment and discipline, adapting strategies to changing circumstances, and cultivating holistic well-being, individuals can achieve financial independence, pursue personal fulfillment, and lead a life of abundance that encompasses happiness, satisfaction, and prosperity in achieving life goals through disciplined planning, proactive decision-making, and strategic wealth management strategies.

www.ingramcontent.com/pod-product-compliance
Lightning Source LLC
Chambersburg PA
CBHW082117220526
45472CB00009B/2213